❧ Caring For A House ❧

VICTOR MARTINEZ

Acknowledgements

© 1992 Chusma House Publications

ISBN: 0-9624536-4-1

Library of Congress
Catalog Card Number: 91-78241

Publisher:
    Charley Trujillo, Chusma House Publications

Graphic Design and Typography:
    Hiram Duran Alvarez

Cover Art:
    Ramiro Martinez

Printed in The United States

CHUSMA
HOUSE ™
Chusma House Publications
P.O. Box 467
San Jose, CA 95103-0467, (408) 9470958

II

I especially want to thank the editors of the following publications in which these poems first appeared:
El Tecolote: A Letter From My Mother, We; Mango: Brothers; ZYZZYVA: National Geographic; High Plains Literary Review: Mistakes; Quarry West: All Is Well; The Berkeley Poetry Review: The Ledger; The Pacific Review: What We Find, The Tumors of Night, Don't Forget; Bloomsbury Review: Bankruptcy; Centro America en el Alma: Caring For A House, The Seed Must Kill, A Thirst For Distance; San Francisco Poetry Issue: The Closet; Tonantzin: Poesía, Shoes; Guadalupe Cultural Arts Center Newsletter: Going Home; Red Trapeze: After Work.

Table of Contents

III

DEDICATED TO
TINA ALVAREZ ROBLES

Chapter I

KEEPING FAITH

When a blister of pus wombs with a furnace
and a cough twists wildly inside a lung,
when nothing is left of the galaxies but a smoke
of crushed promises, remember
that in the distance
there are birds, keeping faith. Their angling caws
fire against the lashes of the sun's ferocious eye —
so don't despair, don't give in.

The earth may be your mother, and you her
favorite child. She may guide you through
the birth scars and rooted blue tendons of the sky
and it may be you who always sleeps
in the warm bed of her palm. But remember this

and make no mistake, one day it will be you
who must give up everything
and slip on those tiny wings; it will be you
who will twitter feebly against the storm, holding up
the horizon until light salts your eyelids
and you awake—
finally, you awaken to a world seen
through the wonder of the earth's two hands, warm
against your cheeks, so that everywhere you turn
your lungs will walk on air.

THE TUMORS OF NIGHT

In this world you must crouch up close to the night.
You have to be there, unafraid, like an eunuch
spiking the King's ear with sarcastic criticisms.
If there's one rule, it's to talk about the cyclops at
the door, or that certain meat in the general's
culinary paté.
Don't bother chewing the fat around your miseries,
the slipped disc entering its crevice of pain
or sniffling about skin
being the braille of a wrong idea.
You must state, simply, and without recourse
to poetry your wonder at being alive simply
alive,
and not whimper your suicidal relief that nothing, only
nothing, exists.
A man, or woman, is not free
who does not let the mess of this world smudge
their clothes. So quit sighing about the weariness
of creation, give up your divine swim
in the ocean's shitted mouth
and keep the migrant birds that arrow the sky with honks
and
twitters, alive, keep them alive, suspended
on your breath, because all you've got is
this leaf of flame, under a sky that purples and pouts
in the gnarled tumors of night.

NO

Sometimes you just know, you can't see it, really,
or describe it in problem-sets or industrial charts
and yet some days you just know the little girl
whose heart is an ashtray stuffed with her father's
cigarettes won't ever come out from under the days
piling up in her like spoiling fish.

Don Alonso isn't going to marvel at Spring again, Tia
Betty
can't stop the weeds of cancer from spreading,
and it's only a matter of hours before Juan's proud knife
kneels to its master.
You just know, that's all, and live,
and hope the war ends, hope the disease that took so
many
won't come smashing through the door and start on you.

Then again they may all have been saved once,
not by the invention of an endless, refillable spoon,
but when you didn't smash the toad by accident
and freed the butterfly meshed on the screen door,
saved, by the light of morning
stuttering away from the trees, even though you know
they are the same trees the gang took Mary
to show her a different Bible.

Another day passes, then another. Each
is a more perfect globe, a more precise reminder
of what no one ever meant to be but perhaps
just is, because we're born by the agreement
of never saying, No.

RAIN

When clouds send rain to count everything they own
every pore opens, every window breathes with the blur
of animals, thinking.
Cars hiss along the blooded teeth of neon.
So click the radio dead, dot the television black, and listen
instead, to the soft sucking of soil
under a dialect of leaves, listen
as clouds scribble notes for the music of sky.

There's no sadness, no fingers weeping through the leaves.
There's only a mouth through which the wind
sings; it is a hat tumbling down the street.

Rain, clattering on the slat-board fences,
curving under eyebrows and smacking foreheads
with the warm milk of memory's tit.
Down your chest and thighs, down your legs it
pours the salt of history
to chill along the sidewalk and waterfall
into a gutter.
                    And then it swells, and waters move.
Business kneels to its mud and houses built on trust
fly down the slopes on the tips of its wing—
even you, there listening
to the excited tongues of the elm tree know
that every last breath of dust you own
will return to the forests from where you came.

WHERE YOU WALK

There are mornings when I swim among the gardens
of marigold. Mornings when birds spin
and snip butterflies off the sun's blistering rim,
and there's no pain greater than to be alive.

Air warms, it wants to feed on my whole length
with slow, pleasurable mandibles
and one day I know it will
when the breath inside me is no longer a need
but the sweet arithmetic of a life
multiplied by many trees, by deep friendships
with rain and sturdy companions among the stars.

But of course this will never happen, because there are
no marigolds. And the hours
I should have let slip deliciously through my nostrils
now sting to the smell of air spoiled over
by intestines blown open by the knife.

There is a pain greater than to be alive.
The slaughterhouses of the rich shrill with their business.
Rain and trees will never be my friends.
Like tumors of small regret
stars will grit their teeth inside me,
and I can't refuse... I can't deny them,
they know where I walk and where I live.

MISTAKES

Mistakes as perfect as the sudden veer
on the freeway, when car brakes sink
and metal and flesh embrace in dance
are even now being inked in the newspapers,
their measurements cut
in the black blood of print.

Equations of X's and Y's are what the earth computes
when making a grave for fear.
They equal the dice of what's to happen
tumbling inside an airplane
about to crash. They are as stealthy as the faults
of kitchen cutlery, as devoted to us as cancer.

There's nothing to pull back
once the hand is sheared by the bandsaw
but still one must try;
because it's possible—sure!—it's possible
to change the slate and register.
But foul-ups still mess the works.

You chew coffee grounds that chance let slip
through the filter, you swim in the green snotty
phlegm of the sea, a sperm wiggling
through the rudiments of dust,
while hope spoils around you just as time spoils
in every minute the fish are left out.

So there's no use praying
for other worlds, for the graded spindles

of things simplified.
The spike of crude error is pocking the distance
between us. A virus of senility is serving out
the purposes of history in a cough,
pushing all catastrophes into the air,
so we can all be touched, all blessed
by those eloquent words space has for saying,
Here, no one needs you.

BANKRUPTCY

No matter what our fortunes tell,
dirt will always be there to receive us.
We are all going to end up sketches
the earth doodles, absentmindedly.

But there are people who already have worms
mewing inside them, people who are born above
the receding thirst of topsoil, or inside
the cavity of a lead pencil—people, so illegible,
they scarcely make a scratch on a page.

But of course—and don't deny it—a world can end
on the cough of a razor, or inside a forehead yawning
to the utter boredom of a bullet.
But that's only a world, the flaming hoax of a snapshot
that will yellow and enter into the mouths of plants
because life itself, continues—
chomping and chomping
its teeth biting the humblest shoe.

FOR JUST THIS MOMENT, I'M SAFE

It's the twin luck of dice that has kept cancer
from snuggling inside me. Even from their crap-out eyes
peek the fear that clenched my breath
and pulled me back inches from a landslide in Huautla.

Away from the black shards that pin me under the sun,
away from this ink and bottomless paper there is some
thing
protecting me, some thing allowing me
to hand over hand
follow the rope of my flesh through.

Of course the ghost of an infectious cough still hungers
for my lungs, and strong winds disturb the windowpanes
with premonitions, but there's a gun, I know, loaded with
blessings, a corral of wind
where all the bullstickers herd together in peace.

Sometimes it seems that it is only me
breathing. Only me being warned by the countless
childhood alarms of a mother's voice. I hear her dress
sputtering like a candle
in the spaces I leave behind.

But what I want to know is this. To whom do I owe
my tribute? To whom should I give
the salt and water of my voice
when it boils over?

When the flower that menaces to bloom its fire
inside my lungs joins
with the last searing treble of gills
from fish hauled up from sea, who should I thank
for this circuit that kept me whole and everlasting,
even if just for a moment?

SHOES

Out of all our enemies, all the catastrophes of nations
scattered to rubble, plowed over with salt, we still have
the warm friendliness, the unrelenting spirit
of our shoes to console us.

Two bubbles chopped square out of shapeless emptiness
how this invention hisses in a hurry to correct time
pumping little sneezes of sympathy for our tardiness.

Although they owe us nothing, they walk
in many of our dreams, conjuring music
from a vaporous sidewalk or standing
as pure reverence
over the peaceful herds of our dead.

They, who always return back to us faithfully
from every tropic, every desert,
to take up their jobs as stealth for the burglar,
spring under the killer's crouch, courage
for the guerrilla. They guard us
against thistles and thorns, protect us from stone
and unseen disasters of glass.

Wheels mean nothing to the shoe. They are the first
of peasants and would never think to kneel
before any god, or suck up to whatever tablet of the Law.
Ravenous for distance, they supply whole lives
with the loss of a mere heel
yet wear death, only once.

WHAT WE FIND

Just as in our skin, there are slivers of truth
on fire inside our acts, as when kneeling
under furniture and retracing, we search
for a lost earring or some other trifle
that helps join us, with purpose, to each minute
and its number.

But it might as well be hope we look for,
that cloud swift as memory across the horizon
because what we find never really adds up
to the attention we wasted looking.

What we find is always the nothing
that will not turn us from our task.

And when we discover that it was hope
we were searching for all along
and not the earring we never did find
by chance or otherwise,
we lay, tired, all our expectations buried
in the enormous doubt of a second before.

THE CHANCE

Don't lie. Don't say it isn't true. No one really wants
to remember the old, the poor poor old, in their livingrooms
summing up the malice of the clock, or on their beds
of torture, enmeshed in tubes or frozen
in narcotic acceptance.
They are oblivious splinters in our memory
that we forget as quickly
as a baby's hand across a computer keyboard.

These days, count them, these black and white chesspieces.
The one strategy that descends from the heavens
is to ripen us with bruises, to reduce us down, deliciously,
to a panic of arteries and frugal scrutiny over salt
until one fine day we awaken
nestled in the embrace of our weeping mother the clock.

But today, while others are measured out, bit by bit,
I invent the chance that I will go untouched—I mean,
not blur or become sluggish over the dictionary,
or drivel on the paper I am assigned to read.

There are so many regions to be conquered in daydream,
so many sunbeams frolicking off the waters
of my desires, but the truth is
as I always suspected. There's no mantis
that won't kill, no bee that refuses work. And just as seasons
snap gratefully together

and belts of memory circle the tree, one day I too
will slow to the sure resolutions of skin, or perhaps
pause to that sudden stopper of surprise
when unfiltered shit can't cork in the cancerous wine.

The math is simple. This world will clap shut
between two eyelids, and I will sleep with what
nourishes there under the ground.

GRAVITY

I take an animal trail down a sheer hillside
to a rush of trees blurring inside a river.
Gnats spin crazily on coded commands,
scraps of molecule rest on stone, then shoot off
when the first green needles slip through the webbings.

Through echoing splinters of sun
my mind enters the horizon. Clouds whimper
under the scuff of my heel, and I scar
the blue with my leaving.

But I return as I must, to fists of dirt clinging
to roots of an upturned cedar. Seasons
twine beneath the bark and break their hold
and I kneel, touching the years. A sliver of wood
sparks, and I know the pain of gravity
in a globe of blood.

ALL IS WELL

I never need to see myself as I am in the mirror
because nothing breathes there.
I know already every molecule
because it is I who sticks a needle of light
through every pore and threads this life.

I talk into my collar to no one who could listen,
even the walls don't answer, nothing
in four directions, not even wind
nor an emptiness one can lean on or move against—

but then a rope, attached to a window and lashed
onto a wall of midnight, descends.
I see the earth humming in airless space:
a globe on fire, with glaciers sliding into gorges
and valleys puddling with human larvae.
There are skies blown to cloudless shreds,
a crawling locust storm of hunger and disease
moving like wind across a boar's hot bristly hide—

but further down, where the tectonic stitches
burn, I see my mother stepping out the back porch
to hang the laundry. And above her, above
her braided hair, a landslide of nuclear wastes
and unexploded bombs, pinless and ready—

but then my father arrives, and together
they talk. She takes his hand. They kiss.
Two old people—they kiss!—
because all is well.

THE SEED MUST KILL

The future that flares from a pistil is the seed
scorching to earth. While darkness leans
against the wind, and trees arrive
on the lip of distance the sun spreads on the road
for travelers, the seed makes itself known.

It demands water, and so reservoirs open
in a cloud. It discovers navigation in the stars,
begins the spinning journey through an intestine
or on a wing, between the brotherhood of dust
and heaven on a hill of dung.

Sure the moon gives its zero percent
the sun its measure and water its spoon
but the seed is at war with History
that wants to consume it, with Astronomy
that seeks to count its graves.

What does it matter that a man cradles under
a tree and celebrates with worms? Who cares
that ink fails? The seed must keep on
with its endless quarrel between ovule and sperm,
and with crowbar arms peel up the crusts of asphalt

and pop like corn on the sidewalk,
because the tumors of the city must be
destroyed, above all they must
be annihilated.

Chapter II

A LETTER FROM MY MOTHER

My mother writes me in an alphabet born from letters
that bite acid into the leather of her bible.
She stitches commas, dots periods exact as the rules
demand; her exclamations are more resolute than weeds.

My mother sits and writes of funerals that have shrunk
her youth down into a tight clarity of wrinkles.
Her days are shards of sun piercing through the leaf's rage,
a root is her pillow, the skies a dead shore far from
the rains that flung her and my father, directionless.

She talks of prayers unleashed when uncle was handcuffed
to a squad car and lead away to confess his own teeth,
and how father says our masters uptown are lessons
from a bruise. And this is why
happiness is stuck in her throat
by grief and its commanding fist.

Son . . . she says, Hijo . . . and I know that all the sorrows
of what my mother could never stomach
except as children will pour from her hands.
Ink will brood and speak its mind
and each word will be pressed, each letter folded
into those paper angels
that won't protect us ever again.

BROTHERS

Where two dogs quiver and sniff tails
and a girl, her breath hooting, hoses water
up her leg, my father comes home
drunk, bloated on his piss and falls cradled
against the curb, a pile of loose muscles
stinking of traffic exhaust. Even now
he may be locked between an ant's pincers,
or drifting on a butterfly's wing. "Nobody's in
this with me, son," he says. "The money's gone
grey out of my hands, or lays crippled somewhere
far from us." His arm on mine weighs
like a tool, and already I hear worms
discussing near his feet. Into the wilderness
of my father's eyes, the days haul slowly down
the road of his calender. I look at his mouth and taste
the wasted efforts, the gaping tooth of nothing
peeping out, and think, Father, we are brothers,
and if this is the way I too will end, let there be
inside me, as there is in you, a young girl
sewing fiercely on a cloth, and a boy
watching clouds continue in a puddle of rain,
and between them the enormous seed of another
son, neither of us can lift enough to bury.

FAMILY ALBUM

Inside windows, light and distance are seized
by an instant. Here I learned what a sky is
when the waters of blue expand, learned clouds
bruising the horizon
is what is meant by rain.
In a polaroid, my aunt
stiffened by cancer stares into a camera as though
it were the ticket out of the hell and misery
scorching inside her Sunday dress.
In a snapshot my father feeds every last molecule
of sweat to the houses he loves.
And there I am, in clothes that have
already lived my brother's life.
I can't help it, but my eyes drizzle to see a home
reduced to a square, and above it, the clouds
going on their way, saying nothing
under their immense reservoirs of light.

THE TIMEKEEPING UNIT

When morning drifts in through the gauze curtains
a body, that all night lay buried in dream
becomes me, testing its weight, sloshing back and forth
the sweet nutrients of daylight, the dual compliments
of push and pull. I'm skin, and there's no denying.
I pucker to a wound and chill
as tomorrow's wind
arrives in the current of yesterday's cold.

A huge hand lowers from the clouds, and tapping my head,
leads me to work, to an office where I hang my coat, unsleeve
my pale sunless arms and dip
into pools of numbers that seeth to a boil
as though needing only flesh to rise from a simmer.

My job is to grapple with timecards, attendance rosters and
mute dumb barrels of basic arithmetic that lumber
over my desk whether I am here or not.
And because I'm afraid
the big boys upstairs will forget me, my necktie drifts
in a current of nervous cigarette smoke.

Sometimes it happens that a boss pulls a lever
and all our promotions shutter
and adjust one more plate. Other times it's like Copeland
who retired with a joke Timex watch and gin-inspired
luncheon speeches. "It's all so unexpected", he said, "suddenly,
you're old."

None of us imagines Copeland's arms

in a walking square, none of us sees him being dealt
furiously beyond the decimal, become a living subtraction
shrinking down into the sediment of those final
disconnected years, when no one will recognize him
and he won't recognize anyone;
because the only light we know for sure
is what streams through these rosters
and never comes back.

AFTER WORK

After work I can barely lift my arms
so sogged are they from damming up the sludge
of numbers. A tiny glacier
slides down over my mouth
and seals it shut.

I begin to walk—home, of course—with first misery
then happiness shifting from one foot to another.
Distance smolders
in the charred bread of my legs.

What promises stretch out on the horizon
what leaps across the circuit of a mirror
to confirm who I am, I don't know.
I only know that when I arrive home,
I take off my coat, and see the wall-clock
and family portraits
that sting my legs
like splinters shot through every pore—

all the room is so perfectly correct, so blissfully
faultless, that my legs want to run
but instead choke into hoarse sobs.

POESIA

She props the blue dress shyly over her shoulders,
sheers a pencil line of mascara and smooths blush
over the cheek hot oil scalded to a smeary wax
at four, then high-heels to the dance.
There the girls lull by the band until one
by one the boys pick them.
Aisles and walls empty, a hum of shadows
murmurs by a door, but no one asks her to dance.
No one asks her name.
A few boys, the ones out of school or out of work
look as if...but it is always 'as if.'
When she leaves the music stutters to a final note
and lays broken beneath the dancer's feet.
Her best friend Sarah loves her. But even she
reddens to watch the smile that sinks
into a grin, the scar for an eyelash. Finally
she quits going anywhere. When Sarah calls she says
water is boiling, a baby cousin
crying, the T.V., important.
But one night, when the house ticks quietly to sleep
and the rooms a warm darkness, she picks up
the mascara pencil and instead of groceries, writes:
"And her eyes will never know what's equal, one to one."
Then folds towels, lines dishes
and presses clothes for tomorrow.
In bed now, under the reading lamp, she takes the pencil
again, and in one motion, writes:
"The landslide of her face will bury them all in the end."
Then she smiles, the smile seared into a grin;
she blinks the blink sudden as a falling lash,
and knows she will go on, morning will come.

GOING HOME

Don't believe it, you can go home,
your footsteps net
the same geometry
on the same frozen grass.
And as though you were fitted
inside a gaze
that had lost you, there
you'll find your family: mother
knit in a dream
where milk pours down endlessly
from a cloud, father
led home again from the foundry
on a leash, brother
hugging his stone because he has
no friends, and sister
her eyes big as wheels
over a cosmetic kit.
And there you are, trailing
the scent of migrations
in textbooks, sticking needles
into insects for display,
taking measures of the trees
who turn to you
the backs of their leaves.

THE CLOSET

The only proof of my uncle is his shoes.
Gone from the heel
is the life he walked as a man.

Not much is left of my aunt's old dress.
From so much darkness
the colors shrunk into the fibers.

It's become nothing now without her:
the shoulders no longer turn
in the sun, the hems lag,
the breasts are vacant and sad.

There are clothes inside a closet
that want to take us over.
Without seed or flesh, they want to continue
a life of hat-sizes, shoe-lengths
and widths of collar.

There's no measure, it's true:
not in man, not in woman.
There's only shoes, a dress, or a tie
that once said, 'You were here!'

DON'T FORGET

When I see my aunt's old dress in the closet
where the soft tissues of her leaving even now
drift in the vacant air, and when I remember
how my grandmother's back would
not let the coffin lid close, the sutures
of my heart unpluck and their lives spill
warm as urine through my arteries.

If one day I let my memory rust
around the milk my mother worked so hard for
in the fields, I know fire will seize the walls
of my heart and gut both the rooms of my lungs.
I know I will be nothing, nothing
but an arrogant head
pushing my way through calendars, searching
for clusters of ovaries to harvest.

RUDOLFO

When my uncle came home from all day delivering
his ear to the village whore, his head to vinegar in a jar,
he would leave the last step of his wandering behind him
on the doormat, along with the stump of his leg,
and in ritual sit on the couch to wind and unwind
absence like a rope between his fingers, or play with
the string of smoke extinguished from his candle.
And then, because his ears had been finely strung
for sound, he would listen for the hymns of rain
on the dust roads leading out of town, for the gruff stalls
of planes overhead in the clouded press.
Artillery meant to scatter his flesh
set free the five fingers of his senses.
He moved slowly toward the light of doors since, and then
without direction, as though unsure of where
to look for the glove lost from its brother.
Yet his head never surrendered its peace, his lips never
broke into storm or common babble he was such a quiet
witness against, although the words were there
scuffed in asphalt—enough words to threaten everyday
to finish him to reduce his life down to those insignificant
advertisements in thin pencil that we would see
at the Surplus Store, above the empty canteens.

SOMETHING TO LIVE FOR

First the car died, its paint
scrubbed twice by summer and
blistered to a stubborn grey,
then the dog you loved so much
and finally you, my uncle, a life
unpacked from a suitcase,
home of four secret pouches.
The jobs that kept you floating
never touched bottom,
your only deeds of ownership
were tinfoil picture frames,
snapshots of those who don't
live now except in me
and then only a moment
or two in the mirror.
You knew more of the ways of birds
than airliners, more in miles walked
than distances of a world
now measured in hours.
The fist you didn't throw
was your word. But why go on?
Let it just be those afternoons
we'd watch birds unlink and sliver off
to join in a chorus of leaves.
Let it be the stories so true
you kept them buried in your pockets
as when the rifle felt
like no weight you ever lifted
because the battle plans spun wrong

but who cared, it was something to die for,
one reason good as any
when a man needs to be raised by a hand
greater than his own. You said this
was a mistake. Uncle, you can't feel
this heart hammering
in the heart of the house you loved,
you can't see how the centuries
of thuggery still rush
through the sieves of the clock,
pushing out the hospitable air
with dynasties of stone, a music of steel
over forests, circuits over words and
words clapping us into squares
for each to defend as our own,
but if your life were a razor,
I know, all the newspapers
would be in shreds now.

HOME

When night closes its vault
and a dog lights his leg
to a hubcap
in the park, buried
under a blanket
of newspapers Juan hears
the tastebuds of the nation
humming in a powerline.
Tonight he wishes to surrender
to the malice of the poor
who put their money on the rich
to that man moving always
on the curve of his eyeball.
No tables bristle with feast
no cold sponges quiet
the many tongues of fever
yet the world cannot breath
unless through him, and so
tomorrow he will scuttle
for cans and turn his
face to concrete.
Tonight, Juan is harvesting fire
on the soil of back home,
he is twitching with laughter
over children who will bud
before the first winds
and like weeds grow stubborn
from his absence.
There's an ocean of loneliness
trapped inside the warm

kitchen of his lungs,
and though his shoes may never
root in the asphalt of this
malnourished soil,
the statues in the park
still scold him, saying,
"Go home, and don't come back."

THE LEDGER

I suffer with songs, yet I create them here on earth...
                                        Cuacuahtzin

I waited this long I might as well stay, I said
under my lapel to no one who could listen
and took out my boyhood collection of June bugs
yellow jackets and other species of wing
that slept once in my cotton pillow of alcohol
before freezing into decoration.

I remember baiting abdomens onto needles
to lure all eyes into my glass cases.
I caught salamander and bullfrog
to scuttle in my muddy tank.
And when the hull of a sandcrab was a lesson
in form, the ghost of a shadow on my palm,
its death was mine and I recorded it in my ledger.

In my ledger I wrote how a cat kneels
stiff under the braiding thread of a mouse,
how winds splash the poplar and a sky opens
and pours milk into a river. I was there,
I stated how paralysis froze my grandpa's tongue,
and through it numbed everything. I heard
and wrote down the words of all the men and women
who in his face blurred, until carried away
with the drool in the washbasin.

And because I took account, because I knew how

to put back the words sponged from the slate,
I was his favorite, I was my family's best—
lugging around my book of events,
telling myself over and over into my collar
that this is all there is. This cold, flat
reduction of the living is all there is. And this too
I wrote down, and about the sidewalks glowing
with rain and neons, the streets hissing with cars.

CARING FOR A HOUSE

Being a marriageless grandson, I am condemned
by family counsel to watch over my grandfather's house,
soaked and rotting now
from the years of his weakening neglect.

I arrive to rains scouring the autumn leaves
across the sidewalk and screaming along the gutter
to mold crawling over furniture, unlinking the dust.
Every whisper opens up huge, unexplained cracks
on the walls and ceiling. Nothing makes sense:
a spoon lays near the unflushed toilet,
a blanket and pillow make a bed in the fireplace,
the staircase to the basement rolls out a dark
slavery tongue, and there appear enormous catacombs
under the kitchen linoleum
where a mighty alliance of termites and cockroaches
announce they will rule.

I squeeze my eyelids, and through a blurry harvest of years
see the peculiar slow-motion of clay
that was my grandfather. I see the illness
that numbed his vision of a couch, erased the last sofa
and chair from his memory, dulled his tongue
until every word, every gesture
took flight and abandoned the nest.

As his grandson, I was obligated to keep the family's sweat
alive, keep pushing our history of sighs

through the pink channel of a lung. Instead, I picked out
the acids of gossip
spiraling like worms inside my ears:
the loss of his tongue, these well-mannered clothes,
my crimes of luxury and total failure to keep his
prescriptions. I even spit into a tantrum
when they asked me to attend his funeral.

A man of books, I once studied the distance
between the first dream of amphibians of themselves
on land, to the space module
springing off of Neptune's sluggish gravity.
I read and re-read the diagram
of what I believed was my soul
classified into so many protean fragments.
But instead of winds of prophecy, I was handled clumsily
back and forth, between one god and another.
One probed me as a boy probes a snail with a stick,
another embraced the web of my molecules
like wind through a collapsing house of cards.
In the end, I bore only a glorious hatred
for this mush and fluid
I once marveled as my body.

At my grandfather's, I was eclipsed from any fruit
of nourishment. My clothes began to silt into my skin
and I noticed a pale, nauseous vapor
emitting from me,
as if right then and there all my crimes

were being summoned up in coughing flames.
In truth, I could suffer him no more, so one night
I awakened, silly with fever and sobbing in the oils
of some mysterious grief.
I caught myself murmuring in the blurred voice
of my grandfather, and in a walking hypnosis,
I climbed up his stairs— and there
he was, standing there above me like those statues
poised one step from rubble
and one short of being hurdled into flesh.
The air sputtered with the pain of his voice
on fire, his mouth blooming
as though the sculptor's chisel was still hot
on his useless genitals.

Grasping the lapel of his one good suit, he told me
of his journeys under the moon's bloodless sickle,
of the times he'd adjust the road straight
from his heel, and of the hunger that curls its wings
around a child and binds him forever to a crib.
He confessed his weariness at living forever
in the scattering seeds of flesh, and with a sweep of his arm
all the years of triumph and failure peeled away.
I beheld a parking lot
no one will ever again enter as a garden, witnessed our home
bulldozed into a shopping mall, while the once hungry
and rebellious breaths of my family
offered up the wealth of their minerals
to a church, and on the altars of property.

No surge of remorse awakened in my lungs, no falling
or rising inside, as when justice landslides
and dignity can only scaffold the ruins.
Instead, I looked down at the snare that once waited for him
now waiting for me, the stone
that would strip down my skin.
And like two great boulders under the ocean,
we clocked our heads, one on another;
light curled on our tongues, and there was no need for eyes.

CHAPTER III

ALPHABET

Out in the blue syringe of afternoon, among the cataract
clouds and blustering eucalyptus, the day
isn't all bliss and morning-glories; it isn't all
nuded trees rising in a praise to form. No, the day
is a page written up: cars in conjunction and
people-periods behind a desk
or as scraps of adjective swarming the sidewalks.

The year is a book which can never be read
the same way twice.
You open its pages and thirst crowds in the breathless
soil of Africa. You close its pages
and there you are, a tiny decimal
surrounded by zeros
that will never multiply nor bruise the world.

You open the book's pages again, and locusts pop
like seed to rain down desert
over the last green jewels. You close its pages
and there you are again, standing
by a window
just as you've stood by a window for these many
years, looking out and waiting—
a statue looming forever out to sea you wait
for this age to ignite ink in your spine
so you can curl into alphabet and be done with it.

THERE IS NO MORE

Under nerves peddling to the music of clouds, the shock
of neons nagging to be fed, there's a story that equals
the sum of everyone else's story, and it's us, at night,
walking through the concrete currents of the city.

Wind drags the scalding gravel of asphalt under our heels,
and above us stars blister with their pitiless
coughs of eternity.
I'm the weight of every last ounce of rubble
quarried in newspaper accounts;
you're a sliver of light
hungering at the lip of a furnace.

But night enriches our embers with dry echoes
of a scorching wind, and when morning arrives
with the sound of error
in the distant crack of two cars, we know it comes
to suture us both inside the wound
of one sleep, join our breaths into one sigh, one hope
that no worry can stunt
into the minutes of the past.

Until we wreck it back to trees and stone
the city exists; it exists as sure as we are weight
pressing these shoes, as sure as we have
already lost to history
all we've ever earned as skin.

Release the keys from their obligation to the door
and like black birds applauding the air
they will come back. Shut off the engines of our books
and they will start up again.
To inhabit that territory of rain
where all the tiny mouths of plants and earth open
so we can drink. That is our chore. That will be
enough. There is no more.

NATIONAL GEOGRAPHIC

I don't want to remember names. Names stink of money, grease,
baby vomit and new clothes. Some stink of righteousness and
patriotism, others of sour deodorant and sweat.
Better to think of heaven: the boiling clouds, the light
like needles sticking into everything,
all the beasts so peaceful and tame.

Don't think it's safe walking when the sign says WALK.
Don't think you'll get by on rent and food.
Just when you think you've got it, just when the dice
tap in line, all hell starts shooting up inside your anatomy.
Organs collapse, skin loosens to the pinch, burn spots
from a gagging liver begin to sprout everywhere,
everything is rocking on ice, shifting on plates
and avalanching down a crotch.
Your heart's beating itself to death.

See that dog? That's a devil dog. It hates you.
It wants to scour your leg with cancer, pluck out your
ligaments, it wants to ignite arthritis in your spine.
And don't put your finger out, don't dare put your finger out,
because the pigeons are eating meat now, and the baby calf
suckled on milk and kept tender in total darkness
is buying a gun. Inside books
the trees are plotting revenge.

Something's happened to the world for sure. Sparrows flop
off trees, choking on diesel fumes, squirrels
stagger around like drunks, from pesticides, from children's

candy. Rats, not landlords, are the true bosses here.
They wrestle the plate from your hands.
They shoot like bullets from one sewer of the city to another.
And don't jerk them around. Smash one and
tomorrow you got eight brothers, ready to settle accounts.
And no amount of talking's gonna spring you loose.
They've got the logic of prison lawyers. They've got
Shakespearean voices. They'll live to see
the last morning in your eyes, die.

Whatever happened to free animals, free trees, free skies?
They all got harnesses on them now.
They're all pulling the big post-industrial plow,
or attached to pullies and curtains and floodlights.
They're props on a stage that's gonna crash down on everybody.

Whatever happened to nice guys, nice girls?
Whatever happened to people who care?
Everybody's in the business of Major Hurt.
He splatters a bloody, betrayed razor in the toilet.
She combs her hair that a cockroach will later sip
between its mandibles. He's got a Master's Degree
in Suffering. She's got a Doctor's in Torture.
Don't mess with this guy, don't mess with her, don't mess,
period. He'll shove a hot needle in your eye, a boll-weevil
in your ear. She'll sponge the whipmarks with salt
and say Now, now, baby, I never meant to hurt you!

But No, you say, No no it ain't so bad!
There's good times, too! Like when an ocean of drugged

happiness floods an orgasm down your legs and out
your shoes and you go splashing big puddles of joy
everywhere, with trees laughing like crazy, the hawk
chuckling, and the bill-collector sleeping
dreaming he's being tortured by a telephone.

Everywhere you go it's Horror Enterprises.
A doorknob gets slimy with fingerprints
from a passing funeral, and still they wipe their asses.
The Exit door to the Terminal Ward closes
and everybody is at home evaporating into a TV.

There're noises at night: a rumble of rubber over tracks.
There're black tears of soot dribbling over the ledge,
traffic signs switching people forward, scarring directions
into the night. There's a gang on the corner
with knifeblades of rumor about you flashing in their palms.
Everybody wants out but still the city keeps
breathing through their pores.

Open the door and the smell of rotting circuits buff against you.
You get plucked, suddenly, one day out of the toilet
by cops dressed as truckdrivers, a shred of shit still dangling
from your ass. No one turns around, no one says anything.
You know you're doomed
when the interrogators turn out to live next door.

But God Bless America! Isn't it great? People will defend
when the time comes. They love it here.
Just don't stare too long at your best friend's T.V.

Don't check out the little white girl with frilly panties
even though it's the taste of her popsickle
you have in your mouth. Stay back! Don't touch
whatever you do!
Because they'll burn every last molecule in your bloodcells.
They'll search out every living hair until they find you.
And when they do, you better take flying lessons, homeboy,
you better have wings.

A THIRST FOR DISTANCE

When I see faces on the freeway hammering with a desire
to kill, and the bolted looks of those determined
to stand watch over their houses, I know these days
are mine, and like the measure
no longer forbidden to measure itself, I am weighed,
and not one ounce of me comes up short.

It's not the grand orchestration of the universe I want
nor the freedom to thread my arrivals
over everyone else's footsteps;
nor is it the simple math of living, the peaceful equation
of setting the clock five minutes ahead
or feeling euphoria over a measly work well done.

I want a life where with one exquisite press
of my shoe I can crush that worm, that magnificent
little comma
always nestled under my heel.
Then I know the markings will no longer signal
a house, a geometry of streets. Then I will see clouds
and more clouds, swoons of gardens
in the drunken air, and oh, the sunlight, I don't want
to forget the sunlight
oozing its syrup over the trees, and everything so
sweet, as I thirst
on the horizon, for distances to open.

EVICTED FROM THE PLANET

When the landlord with the scratch of his key
changed the rivulet from which small spurts of money
trickled, I gave up my studies of insects and migratory
birds and turned instead
to the aimless wander of a cockroach
and boredom squeezing a yawning tear
from the kitchen faucet.

You may be surprised, you may say I lie, or that I didn't
stiffen my fists enough, but as I saw my prints
vanish into a washcloth, saw a vacuum
erase along with my fingernails whatever sweat
glued this room together, whatever worry over back rent
I paced into the carpet, I began slowly
to inhale wisdom
as though all the lies, all the ornaments and tinsel
that decorate our hope and tickle our Christmas trees to
laughter were slothing down my shoulders
and disappearing between the grains of asphalt.

Every atom a lung needs to set its pace toward the stars
became mine. I discovered rains drilling the streets
with acids of bluish ink. I beheld the leaden weight of dreams
people carry like nightshirts to their beds
and felt as my heels lifted
and the globe beneath me spun away
the grieving upsurge of their sobs and misery
backing up all the way to the wingblades of their shoulders.

Hail neons! You ulcers on parade; you little gods of money
bobbing in ether. The pores of the buildings breath
with business, but I circulate nowhere. No breaths
of color cling and smell my clothes; no signs or footsteps
utter the scent of where I've been
or what I've done.
Upwards I rise, above the great scaffolds of the city
triumphant, threading off on stars,
the whole of my life speeding
through the clouds of a nebula.

WE

We reach out to the great snoring blasts of light
and what we embrace is a scorched reminder
of leaves, a season in retreat, with its filthy, unfulfilled
rainbow and sour mornings of regret. And beyond them
uncertainty and fear, scarring the night.

We are nibbling the last of desire down
to its final shredded stalk, and we'll give anything
to be an odor of wet dust, a zero sperm of salt.
Because no one is so correct, we say, that snow cannot
trace winter across their temples, nor slow
the glacial loneliness that surges inside their lungs.

You'll take the clock's two liver-pitted hands,
I'll put on my peasant's shoes.
You'll let the years of your mother's pain
dribble over your shoulder,
I'll be dirt gnawing on the faceless coin,
a sharing of minuses between worms.

But so long as ash doesn't devour what's left of our love,
no urge will dare budge the distance that longs
under our heels. Better the last man, the final woman,
embracing dirt with whatever sweat squeezes
out of our pores, because there's no doubt
we will go—me, you, and all of us swirling down
the funnel where eyes are lost
in the vanishing dimple of the horizon.

GRADUATING FROM STARS

Through stars I learned how suffering
scars the breath I own,
how inside this capsule of clothes, under the studious
curiosity of my collar, I lived
inside the minus of yesterday.

Among stars I always searched for guidance. As I lay,
a few decibels of agreement over a bed, I let their gravity
clutch to the rubble of my face
and in my fingers wound and unwound
the quarrels of my separate faults. First pity then cruelty
opened and closed my fist, then left with the invisible
malice behind a sweet gesture of goodbye.

What bliss to lie porous, like a root or tongue
embedded in the night, listening as voices spiced my ears
with enticing morsals from a heaven
hung on a string. But always I awakened
from this strata of paradise, this echoing stretch of sediment
between now and forever. I awakened, twisted
as though in the bloodless white grip
of a commanding fist, a leaden misery hauling
through every corpuscle
like the weariness of a clock winding down.

Don't ask me why, but the same way one knows that clouds
can be climbed
in the same way as mountains, and that only there
will one find the languages the trees speak, I knew

that this was the house of my youth
collapsing in the square of fire.

So now I no longer let stars swirl my shoes
with indecision, or dredge me grudgingly through calendars.
Now I mortar in my own logic for summing up
the history of the poor. Now I make the voice
of my own anvil sing with repairs.

So watch me, your pupil. Watch me and
listen, as I say, Today, It is enough! I don't need you!
Today, my health is a fibrous tendon,
a compass needle pulling South.

THE TAXIDERMY SHOP

For a long time I endured the boredom of reading books.
My clothes in thistles of rain, and on a leash to the bullying
commands of the clock, I was hot for those gluey
arguments of science and history, those eloquent prescriptions
for saying, "Cure means staying with the herd
even to the slaughterhouse door."

All the same, it was not until my ribs tasted
their final starved nutrients
while being kicked one day to the sidewalk
by a gang of cops, that all my inheritances of logic
slothed down from my shoulders like useless clay.
All the rigors of therapy and articles of faith that had
laid claim to every molecule
began to yellow like piss inside their precious glass cases.

In truth, I was caught in a mesh of self-inflicted
delirium. Yet I wanted an instrument
that could register a precise
and torturous set of calculations
for every wrong decision, and so I consumed clusters
of numbers, and studied the hidden wisecracks
in the mathematical pranks of the universe.
For years I lived happily under the tyranny of this faith,
undisturbed by longing and yet quarreling
through every microbe. I tracked the spore of desire
down to its source and burned it
with a long and unrelenting drought.

Cold air shimmered with mystery and drizzles of regret
when the warmth of those everlasting fires began to escape
from me—
some days in quiet, uneventful spurts,
other days with a fantastic hissing and exhaustion.
And so, someone I believe was me
dragged a body out into the street; its pockets stuffed
with gadgets for describing the migrations of textbooks,
measuring devices for double-helixing the musical
principles of molecules, and other
less reliable gizmos for trapping space or gauging regions
where evolution could be knocked
into reverse, or set free on its own.

I knew with these tools I could weave together any fool's
paradise. And so I amazed everyone with the simple
contraptions of a mere trick, an equation, really,
whereby slipping words into the sleeve of a proposition
then grafting them to the memory
of how my mother advanced me, ungrammatic, into the dark,
became the light that parallels the Self
until it hooks with creation.

I could have settled right then and there to be a clown,
a government stoolie or fool
stroking the corporate hand. Instead, I convinced everyone
of the need for Truth, and of my exalted place
within that quest.
I discovered methods to prolong the importance of costumes,
crunched out irrefutable formulas
for the need of a make-believe heaven.

In those days my disciples were a dwarf I once saved

from being pinned forever under a wastebasket,
also a woman I photographed while she laughed
sideways into a mirror.
I called to them, "Follow me!"
and together we roamed the cities of the world,
ministering unto those people who would otherwise be
driven from this earth
mounted on an error.

Then one day our movement died, it all collapsed
from a theoretical fungus in its roots, lack of minerals
or torque, I didn't know.
By mistake we chanced inside a Taxidermy Shop,
that when we entered lit up suddenly
as though a coin were plopped into an arcade machine.

And from those dead pelts we were greeted by a wild
chorus of roars, of grunts and snortings—
whole volleys of cackles spewed from the mounts of birdless
feathers—
and we were stunned and crippled
by how much of our most sacred pronouncements,
our most privileged decrees, came bursting and bursting
from those animals
locked, like us, inside their own ashes.

ALONG THE RIVER

There are sunrises where everything that pains us, leaves.
Where one's arm twisted on a question
unravels its answer, and the fraction of a face becomes whole.

The sun blossoms shards of glass opposites everywhere
yet none of them touches us.
We are in a forest gummed together by light,
beside a river whose currents are feathers
twittering to become wind
before the sun shreds them madly to their source.

And after the seedless sowing of late afternoon shadows,
when the forest moves at the speed the sun pulls
we say, This
is what I am: a sky of frightened birds,
an unmapped constellation of pores,
morning and night
forever stroking the wheel with each hand—
sun, moon, all the rest.

ONE DAY MORE, ANOTHER DAY LESS

Once, when my breath was a netted sinew
of laughter seizing the wind, my teeth
a bite that spilled back from a plum
spotted with a night of stars, I believed air
would always buff with the odor of disturbed spices,
believed that a slip of hills would always blaze
in the distance. Now pillows of doubt
throttle through these cramped vessels, and though
earth has yellowed and nourished greatly
with my sweat, I find myself shivering sometimes
under the immense shadow of a word, my lungs
blossoming with thistles.
This isn't the touch of seed I always hoped for,
but a world in which the square rules, the circle
defeats, and my only triumph is of strippng back
and composing in memory
every last joyful salt and stubborn grain
of uncompromised bread, while every morning
the sky issues its measure,
one day more, another day less.

IN THE FEVER OF MEMORY

Kneeling beside you there's no need to ask
if you would return with me and together
we could find that night, flattening
on the wind of a fathomless cloud, that alley
where the scent of oil broke over our tongues
and scores were settled and crowned with scabs.
Do you remember those years of trees
clenching the horizon, and clouds bullying their way
across, bringing rain that tasted of salt?
Do you remember how our skin couldn't help
but brawl for another life, another neighborhood
where air wasn't sweetened with the fear
of those who got what they deserved?
If I, because you wish, create a world for you,
you must come here. Because no one lives
at the address you've kept all these years,
no one sleeps on your bed. Instead of a body,
there's the weight of a wrong no one can lift.
There's me, who will never forget, leaning
beside your bed, my hand squeezing the pulse
of your hand, because I love you so much...
because I hate you...

BELIEVING

When I found myself groping for that one ounce of joy
buried under the great slab weights of scorn
I knew believing was not far behind.
It is what sews my button, irons my shirt;
it is my sudden panic
that all the tidy little corrections
will come unseamed.

Out on the street, the sutures pop from the left half
of my smile, but still I believe.

I've yet to become that dog, lapping up the infectious
puddles of patriotism, or that rat
sucking on the holy holy god of the dollar,
but I am definitely that horse, mounted with an immense
saddle of sweat, and every morning
I gallop to the horizon's end,
that sweet nipple of distance
that vanishes
even before I arrive.